That Gratitude Guy's Daily Gratitude Journal

**David George Brooke
That Gratitude Guy**

Copyright © 2021 David George Brooke. All rights reserved. No portion of this book may be reproduced mechanically, electronically, or by any other means, including photocopying, without written permission of the publisher. It is illegal to copy this book, post it to a website, or distribute it by any other means without permission from the publisher.
David George Brooke
4189 W. Lake Sammamish Pkwy SE #B309
Bellevue, WA 98008
206-371-8309
david@thatgratitudeguy.com
http://www.thatgratitudeguy.com
ISBN: 979871334064

Limits of Liability and Disclaimer of Warranty

The author and publisher shall not be liable for your misuse of this material. This book is strictly for informational and educational purposes.

Warning – Disclaimer

The purpose of this book is to educate and entertain. The author and/or publisher do not guarantee that anyone following these techniques, suggestions, tips, ideas, or strategies will become successful. The author and/or publisher shall have neither liability nor responsibility to anyone with respect to any loss or damage caused, or alleged to be caused, directly or indirectly, by the information contained in this book.

In case this journal is lost, please return to:

Name: _____

Phone #: _____

E-Mail: _____

Dedication

To anyone looking for a healthy coping mechanism to help you navigate the trials and tribulations of life.

Contents

Acknowledgements	i
1) How to use this Journal	13
2) Daily Entries	15 - 202
3) About the Author	204
4) Note Pages	205 - 207

Acknowledgements

Connor Brooke, Kyle Brooke, Bob Crosetto, Jim Rio, Walt Miller, Mark Davis, Mark Caton, Scott Burns, Rand McMeins, Gary Blackbourn, Kris Sundberg, Rob Brooke, Don Brooke & Gina Marcell

Everyone needs something that can direct, inspire,
and empower them to move forward every day.
There is tremendous power in living with gratitude.
This gratitude journal will change your life, and after all…
if you want to change your life… "Change your life."
Recording your gratitude thoughts and feelings will
reinforce them in your mind even further every day.

"If you think about it, it's like a dream,
If you talk about it, it inspires you, but,
If you write about it, it empowers you."

~ David George Brooke

How to use
That Gratitude Guy's
Daily Gratitude Journal

Enter the Day & Date:
Write the day and date for your daily gratitude journal entry.

Daily Number
Record your "daily number" which is between 1 and 10. Your daily number describes your current "frame of mind" and enables you to track your feelings/attitudes from one day to the next. 1 is you are experiencing one of your toughest days ever, and 10 is one of the best days of your life. Enter the "before" number before you write in your journal. After writing, enter your "after" number in the lower right-hand corner, and note if your number has changed.

Current Events & Special Occasions
List any special event or significant occurrence that you may want to reference at a later time.

GRATITUDE TODAY
Record the first thoughts that come into your mind. Try to consciously list items in order of greatest importance. Be aware of your health, your family, your friends, your relationships, your job, your home, and maybe just the fact you got to take a hot shower this morning.

Highlight or Anticipated Highlight of the Day
List something that was the most memorable aspect of your day or something you are looking forward to. This will help you to focus on a positive event in the past or present 24 hours.

GRATITUDE FOR TOMORROW
This is everything you are *going* to be grateful for. As your mind focuses forward, an intentioned mind will direct itself toward your future thoughts of gratitude.

GRATITUDE TODAY

Day: _____

Date: _____

Daily # (Before): _____

Current Events/Special Occasion:

_____

_____

I am grateful for:

_____

_____

_____

_____

_____

_____

_____

The highlight or anticipated highlight for my day:

_____

_____

Feeling gratitude and not expressing it is like wrapping a present and not giving it. ~ William Arthur Ward

GRATITUDE FOR TOMORROW

_____ Daily # (After): _____

GRATITUDE TODAY

Day: _____

Date: _____

Daily # (Before): _____

Current Events/Special Occasion:

_____

_____

I am grateful for:

_____

_____

_____

_____

_____

_____

_____

The highlight or anticipated highlight for my day:

_____

_____

The single greatest thing you can do to change your life today would be to start being grateful today. ~ Oprah Winfrey

GRATITUDE FOR TOMORROW

_____ Daily # (After): _____

GRATITUDE TODAY

Day: _____

Date: _____

Daily # (Before): _____

Current Events/Special Occasion:

_____

_____

I am grateful for:

_____

_____

_____

_____

_____

_____

_____

_____

_____

The highlight or anticipated highlight for my day:

_____

_____

Silent gratitude isn't much use to anyone. ~ G.B. Stern

GRATITUDE FOR TOMORROW

_____ Daily # (After): _____

GRATITUDE TODAY

Day: _____

Date: _____

Daily # (Before): _____

Current Events/Special Occasion:

_____

_____

I am grateful for:

_____

_____

_____

_____

_____

_____

_____

_____

The highlight or anticipated highlight for my day:

_____

_____

If the only prayer you said in your whole life was, "Thank you," that would suffice. ~ Meister Eckhart

GRATITUDE FOR TOMORROW

_____ Daily # (After): _____

GRATITUDE TODAY

Day: _____

Date: _____

Daily # (Before): _____

Current Events/Special Occasion:

_____

_____

I am grateful for:

_____

_____

_____

_____

_____

_____

_____

The highlight or anticipated highlight for my day:

_____

_____

There is no such thing as gratitude unexpressed. If it is unexpressed, it is plain, old-fashioned ingratitude. ~ R. Brault

GRATITUDE FOR TOMORROW

_____ Daily # (After): _____

GRATITUDE TODAY

Day: _____

Date: _____

Daily # (Before): _____

Current Events/Special Occasion:

_____

_____

I am grateful for:

_____

_____

_____

_____

_____

_____

_____

_____

The highlight or anticipated highlight for my day:

_____

_____

Gratitude is the memory of the heart. ~ Jean Baptiste Massieu, translated from French

GRATITUDE FOR TOMORROW

_____ Daily # (After): _____

GRATITUDE TODAY

Day: _____

Date: _____

Daily # (Before): _____

Current Events/Special Occasion:

_____

_____

I am grateful for:

_____

_____

_____

_____

_____

_____

_____

_____

The highlight or anticipated highlight for my day:

_____

_____

When we were children we were grateful to those who filled our stockings at Christmas time. Why are we not grateful to God for filling our stockings with legs? ~ G. K. Chesterton

GRATITUDE FOR TOMORROW

_____ Daily # (After): _____

GRATITUDE TODAY

Day: _____

Date: _____

Daily # (Before): _____

Current Events/Special Occasion:

_____

_____

I am grateful for:

_____

_____

_____

_____

_____

_____

_____

The highlight or anticipated highlight for my day:

_____

_____

The only people with whom you should try to get even are those who have helped you. ~ John E. Southard

GRATITUDE FOR TOMORROW

_____ Daily # (After): _____

GRATITUDE TODAY

Day: _____

Date: _____

Daily # (Before): _____

Current Events/Special Occasion:

_____

_____

I am grateful for:

_____

_____

_____

_____

_____

_____

_____

_____

The highlight or anticipated highlight for my day:

_____

_____

Gratitude is an art of painting an adversity into a lovely picture. ~ Kak Sri

GRATITUDE FOR TOMORROW

_____ Daily # (After): _____

GRATITUDE TODAY

Day: _____

Date: _____

Daily # (Before): _____

Current Events/Special Occasion:

_____

_____

I am grateful for:

_____

_____

_____

_____

_____

_____

_____

The highlight or anticipated highlight for my day:

_____

_____

As each day comes to us refreshed and anew, so does my gratitude renew itself daily. ~ Terri Gauteet

GRATITUDE FOR TOMORROW

_____ Daily # (After): _____

GRATITUDE TODAY

Day: _____

Date: _____

Daily # (Before): _____

Current Events/Special Occasion:

_____

_____

I am grateful for:

_____

_____

_____

_____

_____

_____

_____

_____

The highlight or anticipated highlight for my day:

_____

_____

I would maintain that thanks are the highest form of thought; and that gratitude is happiness doubled by wonder. ~ G. K. Chesterton

GRATITUDE FOR TOMORROW

_____ Daily # (After): _____

GRATITUDE TODAY

Day: _____

Date: _____

Daily # (Before): _____

Current Events/Special Occasion:

_____

_____

I am grateful for:

_____

_____

_____

_____

_____

_____

_____

The highlight or anticipated highlight for my day:

_____

_____

If a fellow isn't thankful for what he's got, he isn't likely to be thankful for what he's going to get. ~ Frank A. Clark

GRATITUDE FOR TOMORROW

_____ Daily # (After): _____

GRATITUDE TODAY

Day: _____

Date: _____

Daily # (Before): _____

Current Events/Special Occasion:

_____

_____

I am grateful for:

_____

_____

_____

_____

_____

_____

_____

_____

The highlight or anticipated highlight for my day:

_____

_____

The unthankful heart... discovers no mercies; but let the thankful heart sweep through the day and, as the magnet finds the iron, so it will find, in every hour, some heavenly blessings! ~ Henry Ward Beecher

GRATITUDE FOR TOMORROW

_____ Daily # (After): _____

GRATITUDE TODAY

Day: _____

Date: _____

Daily # (Before): _____

Current Events/Special Occasion:

_____

_____

I am grateful for:

_____

_____

_____

_____

_____

_____

_____

The highlight or anticipated highlight for my day:

_____

_____

Grace isn't a little prayer you chant before receiving a meal. It's a way to live. ~ Attributed to Jacqueline Winspear

GRATITUDE FOR TOMORROW

_____ Daily # (After): _____

GRATITUDE TODAY

Day: _____

Date: _____

Daily # (Before): _____

Current Events/Special Occasion:

_____

_____

I am grateful for:

_____

_____

_____

_____

_____

_____

_____

_____

The highlight or anticipated highlight for my day:

_____

_____

Praise the bridge that carried you over. ~ George Colman

GRATITUDE FOR TOMORROW

_____ Daily # (After): _____

GRATITUDE TODAY

Day: _____

Date: _____

Daily # (Before): _____

Current Events/Special Occasion:

_____

_____

I am grateful for:

_____

_____

_____

_____

_____

_____

_____

_____

The highlight or anticipated highlight for my day:

_____

_____

If you count all your assets, you always show a profit. ~ Robert Quillen

GRATITUDE FOR TOMORROW

_____ Daily # (After): _____

GRATITUDE TODAY

Day: _____

Date: _____

Daily # (Before): _____

Current Events/Special Occasion:

_____

_____

I am grateful for:

_____

_____

_____

_____

_____

_____

_____

The highlight or anticipated highlight for my day:

_____

_____

He is a wise man who does not grieve for the things which he has not, but rejoices for those which he has. ~ Epictetus

GRATITUDE FOR TOMORROW

_____ Daily # (After): _____

GRATITUDE TODAY

Day: _____

Date: _____

Daily # (Before): _____

Current Events/Special Occasion:

_____

_____

I am grateful for:

_____

_____

_____

_____

_____

_____

_____

_____

The highlight or anticipated highlight for my day:

_____

_____

What a miserable thing life is: you're living in clover, only the clover isn't good enough. ~ Bertolt Brecht, Jungle of Cities, 1924

GRATITUDE FOR TOMORROW

_____ Daily # (After): _____

GRATITUDE TODAY

Day: _____

Date: _____

Daily # (Before): _____

Current Events/Special Occasion:

_____

_____

I am grateful for:

_____

_____

_____

_____

_____

_____

_____

_____

The highlight or anticipated highlight for my day:

_____

_____

Gratitude is the best attitude. ~ Author Unknown

GRATITUDE FOR TOMORROW

_____ Daily # (After): _____

GRATITUDE TODAY

Day: _____

Date: _____

Daily # (Before): _____

Current Events/Special Occasion:

_____

_____

I am grateful for:

_____

_____

_____

_____

_____

_____

_____

The highlight or anticipated highlight for my day:

_____

_____

Not what we say about our blessings, but how we use them, is the true measure of our thanksgiving. ~ W.T. Purkiser

GRATITUDE FOR TOMORROW

_____ Daily # (After): _____

GRATITUDE TODAY

Day: _____

Date: _____

Daily # (Before): _____

Current Events/Special Occasion:

_____

_____

I am grateful for:

_____

_____

_____

_____

_____

_____

_____

The highlight or anticipated highlight for my day:

_____

_____

We thank Thee, O Father of all, for... all the soul-help that sad souls understand.
~ Will Carleton

GRATITUDE FOR TOMORROW

_____ Daily # (After): _____

GRATITUDE TODAY

Day: _____

Date: _____

Daily # (Before): _____

Current Events/Special Occasion:

_____

_____

I am grateful for:

_____

_____

_____

_____

_____

_____

_____

The highlight or anticipated highlight for my day:

_____

_____

We can only be said to be alive in those moments when our hearts are conscious of our treasures. ~ Thornton Wilder

GRATITUDE FOR TOMORROW

_____ Daily # (After): _____

GRATITUDE TODAY

Day: _____

Date: _____

Daily # (Before): _____

Current Events/Special Occasion:

_____

_____

I am grateful for:

_____

_____

_____

_____

_____

_____

_____

The highlight or anticipated highlight for my day:

_____

_____

Gratitude is a quality similar to electricity: it must be produced and discharged and used up in order to exist at all. ~ William Faulkner

GRATITUDE FOR TOMORROW

_____ Daily # (After): _____

GRATITUDE TODAY

Day: _____

Date: _____

Daily # (Before): _____

Current Events/Special Occasion:

_____

_____

I am grateful for:

_____

_____

_____

_____

_____

_____

_____

_____

The highlight or anticipated highlight for my day:

_____

_____

If you want to turn your life around, try thankfulness. It will change your life mightily. ~ Gerald Good

GRATITUDE FOR TOMORROW

_____ Daily # (After): _____

GRATITUDE TODAY

Day: _____

Date: _____

Daily # (Before): _____

Current Events/Special Occasion:

_____

_____

I am grateful for:

_____

_____

_____

_____

_____

_____

_____

_____

The highlight or anticipated highlight for my day:

_____

_____

Gratitude is the least of the virtues, but ingratitude is the worst of vices.
~ Thomas Fuller

GRATITUDE FOR TOMORROW

_____ Daily # (After): _____

GRATITUDE TODAY

Day: _____

Date: _____

Daily # (Before): _____

Current Events/Special Occasion:

_____

_____

I am grateful for:

_____

_____

_____

_____

_____

_____

_____

The highlight or anticipated highlight for my day:

_____

_____

There is not a more pleasing exercise of the mind than gratitude. It is accompanied with such an inward satisfaction that the duty is done.
~ Joseph Addison

GRATITUDE FOR TOMORROW

_____ Daily # (After): _____

GRATITUDE TODAY

Day: _____

Date: _____

Daily # (Before): _____

Current Events/Special Occasion:

_____

_____

I am grateful for:

_____

_____

_____

_____

_____

_____

_____

_____

The highlight or anticipated highlight for my day:

_____

_____

I feel a very unusual sensation - if it is not indigestion, I think it must be gratitude. ~ Benjamin Disraeli

GRATITUDE FOR TOMORROW

_____ Daily # (After): _____

GRATITUDE TODAY

Day: _____

Date: _____

Daily # (Before): _____

Current Events/Special Occasion:

_____

_____

I am grateful for:

_____

_____

_____

_____

_____

_____

_____

The highlight or anticipated highlight for my day:

_____

_____

There is no greater difference between men than between grateful and ungrateful people. ~ R. H. Blyth

GRATITUDE FOR TOMORROW

_____ Daily # (After): _____

GRATITUDE TODAY

Day: _____

Date: _____

Daily # (Before): _____

Current Events/Special Occasion:

_____

_____

I am grateful for:

_____

_____

_____

_____

_____

_____

The highlight or anticipated highlight for my day:

_____

_____

Courtesies of a small and trivial character are the ones which strike deepest in the grateful and appreciating heart. ~ H. Clay

GRATITUDE FOR TOMORROW

_____ Daily # (After): _____

GRATITUDE TODAY

Day: _____

Date: _____

Daily # (Before): _____

Current Events/Special Occasion:

_____

_____

I am grateful for:

_____

_____

_____

_____

_____

_____

_____

_____

The highlight or anticipated highlight for my day:

_____

_____

Who does not thank for little will not thank for much. ~ Estonian Proverb

GRATITUDE FOR TOMORROW

_____ Daily # (After): _____

GRATITUDE TODAY

Day: _____

Date: _____

Daily # (Before): _____

Current Events/Special Occasion:

_____

_____

I am grateful for:

_____

_____

_____

_____

_____

_____

_____

The highlight or anticipated highlight for my day:

_____

_____

All that we behold is full of blessings. ~ William Wordsworth

GRATITUDE FOR TOMORROW

_____ Daily # (After): _____

GRATITUDE TODAY

Day: _____

Date: _____

Daily # (Before): _____

Current Events/Special Occasion:

_____

_____

I am grateful for:

_____

_____

_____

_____

_____

_____

_____

The highlight or anticipated highlight for my day:

_____

_____

The hardest arithmetic to master is that which enables us to count our blessings.
~ Eric Hoffer

GRATITUDE FOR TOMORROW

_____ Daily # (After): _____

GRATITUDE TODAY

Day: _____

Date: _____

Daily # (Before): _____

Current Events/Special Occasion:

_____

_____

I am grateful for:

_____

_____

_____

_____

_____

_____

_____

_____

The highlight or anticipated highlight for my day:

_____

_____

Gratitude is the fairest blossom which springs from the soul. ~ Henry Ward Beecher

GRATITUDE FOR TOMORROW

_____ Daily # (After): _____

GRATITUDE TODAY

Day: _____

Date: _____

Daily # (Before): _____

Current Events/Special Occasion:

_____

_____

I am grateful for:

_____

_____

_____

_____

_____

_____

_____

_____

The highlight or anticipated highlight for my day:

_____

_____

When our perils are past, shall our gratitude sleep? ~ George Canning

GRATITUDE FOR TOMORROW

_____ Daily # (After): _____

GRATITUDE TODAY

Day: _____

Date: _____

Daily # (Before): _____

Current Events/Special Occasion:

_____

_____

I am grateful for:

_____

_____

_____

_____

_____

_____

_____

The highlight or anticipated highlight for my day:

_____

_____

As we express our gratitude, we must never forget that the highest appreciation is not to utter words, but to live by them. ~ J. F. Kennedy

GRATITUDE FOR TOMORROW

_____ Daily # (After): _____

GRATITUDE TODAY

Day: _____

Date: _____

Daily # (Before): _____

Current Events/Special Occasion:

_____

_____

I am grateful for:

_____

_____

_____

_____

_____

_____

_____

_____

The highlight or anticipated highlight for my day:

_____

_____

We often take for granted the very things that most deserve our gratitude.
~ Cynthia Ozick

GRATITUDE FOR TOMORROW

_____ Daily # (After): _____

GRATITUDE TODAY

Day: _____

Date: _____

Daily # (Before): _____

Current Events/Special Occasion:

_____

_____

I am grateful for:

_____

_____

_____

_____

_____

_____

_____

_____

The highlight or anticipated highlight for my day:

_____

_____

The grateful person, being still the most severe exacter of himself, not only confesses, but proclaims, his debts. ~ R. South

GRATITUDE FOR TOMORROW

_____ Daily # (After): _____

GRATITUDE TODAY

Day: _____

Date: _____

Daily # (Before): _____

Current Events/Special Occasion:

_____

_____

I am grateful for:

_____

_____

_____

_____

_____

_____

_____

_____

The highlight or anticipated highlight for my day:

_____

_____

Gratitude is merely the secret hope of further favors. ~ François Duc de La Rochefoucauld

GRATITUDE FOR TOMORROW

_____ Daily # (After): _____

GRATITUDE TODAY

Day: _____

Date: _____

Daily # (Before): _____

Current Events/Special Occasion:

_____

_____

I am grateful for:

_____

_____

_____

_____

_____

_____

_____

The highlight or anticipated highlight for my day:

_____

_____

Most human beings have an almost infinite capacity for taking things for granted. ~ Aldous Huxley

GRATITUDE FOR TOMORROW

_____ Daily # (After): _____

GRATITUDE TODAY

Day: _____

Date: _____

Daily # (Before): _____

Current Events/Special Occasion:

_____

_____

I am grateful for:

_____

_____

_____

_____

_____

_____

_____

_____

The highlight or anticipated highlight for my day:

_____

_____

Hem your blessings with thankfulness so they don't unravel. ~ Author Unknown

GRATITUDE FOR TOMORROW

_____ Daily # (After): _____

GRATITUDE TODAY

Day: _____

Date: _____

Daily # (Before): _____

Current Events/Special Occasion:

___

___

I am grateful for:

___

___

___

___

___

___

___

The highlight or anticipated highlight for my day:

___

___

God gave you a gift of 86,400 seconds today. Have you used one to say "thank you?" ~ William A. Ward

GRATITUDE FOR TOMORROW

_____ Daily # (After): _____

GRATITUDE TODAY

Day: _____

Date: _____

Daily # (Before): _____

Current Events/Special Occasion:

_____

_____

I am grateful for:

_____

_____

_____

_____

_____

_____

_____

_____

The highlight or anticipated highlight for my day:

_____

_____

Gratitude makes sense of our past, brings peace for today, and creates a vision for tomorrow. ~ Melody Beattie

GRATITUDE FOR TOMORROW

_____ Daily # (After): _____

GRATITUDE TODAY

Day: _____

Date: _____

Daily # (Before): _____

Current Events/Special Occasion:

_____

_____

I am grateful for:

_____

_____

_____

_____

_____

_____

_____

_____

The highlight or anticipated highlight for my day:

_____

_____

I am full of gratitude for my life - and for this house. ~ J. Clary

GRATITUDE FOR TOMORROW

_____ Daily # (After): _____

GRATITUDE TODAY

Day: _____

Date: _____

Daily # (Before): _____

Current Events/Special Occasion:

_____

_____

I am grateful for:

_____

_____

_____

_____

_____

_____

_____

The highlight or anticipated highlight for my day:

_____

_____

Saying thank you is more than good manners. It is good spirituality.
~ Alfred Painter

GRATITUDE FOR TOMORROW

_____ Daily # (After): _____

GRATITUDE TODAY

Day: _____

Date: _____

Daily # (Before): _____

Current Events/Special Occasion:

_____

_____

I am grateful for:

_____

_____

_____

_____

_____

_____

_____

The highlight or anticipated highlight for my day:

_____

_____

Joy is the simplest form of gratitude. ~ Karl Barth

GRATITUDE FOR TOMORROW

_____ Daily # (After): _____

GRATITUDE TODAY

Day: _____

Date: _____

Daily # (Before): _____

Current Events/Special Occasion:

_____

_____

I am grateful for:

_____

_____

_____

_____

_____

_____

_____

_____

The highlight or anticipated highlight for my day:

_____

_____

Nothing is more honorable than a grateful heart. ~ Lucius Annaeus Seneca

GRATITUDE FOR TOMORROW

_____ Daily # (After): _____

GRATITUDE TODAY

Day: _____

Date: _____

Daily # (Before): _____

Current Events/Special Occasion:

_____

_____

I am grateful for:

_____

_____

_____

_____

_____

_____

_____

The highlight or anticipated highlight for my day:

_____

_____

When we give cheerfully and accept gratefully, everyone is blessed. ~ Maya Angelou

GRATITUDE FOR TOMORROW

_____ Daily # (After): _____

GRATITUDE TODAY

Day: _____

Date: _____

Daily # (Before): _____

Current Events/Special Occasion:

_____

_____

I am grateful for:

_____

_____

_____

_____

_____

_____

_____

The highlight or anticipated highlight for my day:

_____

_____

Gratitude for the present moment and the fullness of life now is the true prosperity. ~ Eckhart Tolle

GRATITUDE FOR TOMORROW

_____ Daily # (After): _____

GRATITUDE TODAY

Day: _____

Date: _____

Daily # (Before): _____

Current Events/Special Occasion:

_____

_____

I am grateful for:

_____

_____

_____

_____

_____

_____

_____

_____

The highlight or anticipated highlight for my day:

_____

_____

The best way to appreciate your job is to imagine yourself without one.
~ Oscar Wilde

GRATITUDE FOR TOMORROW

_____ Daily # (After): _____

GRATITUDE TODAY

Day: _____

Date: _____

Daily # (Before): _____

Current Events/Special Occasion:

_____

_____

I am grateful for:

_____

_____

_____

_____

_____

_____

_____

The highlight or anticipated highlight for my day:

_____

_____

We tend to forget that happiness doesn't come as a result of getting something we don't have, but rather of recognizing and appreciating what we do have. ~ Frederick Koenig

GRATITUDE FOR TOMORROW

_____ Daily # (After): _____

GRATITUDE TODAY

Day: _____

Date: _____

Daily # (Before): _____

Current Events/Special Occasion:

_____

_____

I am grateful for:

_____

_____

_____

_____

_____

_____

_____

The highlight or anticipated highlight for my day:

_____

_____

The single greatest thing you can do to change your life today would be to start being grateful today. ~ Oprah Winfrey

GRATITUDE FOR TOMORROW

_____ Daily # (After): _____

GRATITUDE TODAY

Day: _____

Date: _____

Daily # (Before): _____

Current Events/Special Occasion:

_____

_____

I am grateful for:

_____

_____

_____

_____

_____

_____

_____

The highlight or anticipated highlight for my day:

_____

_____

Silent gratitude isn't much use to anyone. ~ G. B. Stern

GRATITUDE FOR TOMORROW

_____ Daily # (After): _____

GRATITUDE TODAY

Day: _____

Date: _____

Daily # (Before): _____

Current Events/Special Occasion:

_____

_____

I am grateful for:

_____

_____

_____

_____

_____

_____

_____

_____

The highlight or anticipated highlight for my day:

_____

_____

If the only prayer you said in your whole life was, "Thank you," that would suffice. ~ Meister Eckhart

GRATITUDE FOR TOMORROW

_____ Daily # (After): _____

GRATITUDE TODAY

Day: _____

Date: _____

Daily # (Before): _____

Current Events/Special Occasion:

_____

_____

I am grateful for:

_____

_____

_____

_____

_____

_____

_____

_____

The highlight or anticipated highlight for my day:

_____

_____

There is no such thing as gratitude unexpressed. If it is unexpressed, it is plain, old-fashioned ingratitude. ~ R. Brault

GRATITUDE FOR TOMORROW

_____ Daily # (After): _____

GRATITUDE TODAY

Day: _____

Date: _____

Daily # (Before): _____

Current Events/Special Occasion:

_____

_____

I am grateful for:

_____

_____

_____

_____

_____

_____

_____

_____

The highlight or anticipated highlight for my day:

_____

_____

Gratitude is the memory of the heart. ~ Jean Baptiste Massieu, translated from French

GRATITUDE FOR TOMORROW

_____ Daily # (After): _____

GRATITUDE TODAY

Day: _____

Date: _____

Daily # (Before): _____

Current Events/Special Occasion:

_____

_____

I am grateful for:

_____

_____

_____

_____

_____

_____

_____

The highlight or anticipated highlight for my day:

_____

_____

When we were children we were grateful to those who filled our stockings at Christmas time. Why are we not grateful to God for filling our stockings with legs? ~ G. K. Chesterton

GRATITUDE FOR TOMORROW

_____ Daily # (After): _____

GRATITUDE TODAY

Day: _____

Date: _____

Daily # (Before): _____

Current Events/Special Occasion:

_____

_____

I am grateful for:

_____

_____

_____

_____

_____

_____

_____

_____

The highlight or anticipated highlight for my day:

_____

_____

The only people with whom you should try to get even are those who have helped you. ~ John E. Southard

GRATITUDE FOR TOMORROW

_____ Daily # (After): _____

GRATITUDE TODAY

Day: _____

Date: _____

Daily # (Before): _____

Current Events/Special Occasion:

_____

_____

I am grateful for:

_____

_____

_____

_____

_____

_____

_____

_____

The highlight or anticipated highlight for my day:

_____

_____

Gratitude is an art of painting an adversity into a lovely picture. ~ Kak Sri

GRATITUDE FOR TOMORROW

_____ Daily # (After): _____

GRATITUDE TODAY

Day: _____

Date: _____

Daily # (Before): _____

Current Events/Special Occasion:

_____

_____

I am grateful for:

_____

_____

_____

_____

_____

_____

_____

The highlight or anticipated highlight for my day:

_____

_____

If you have lived, take thankfully the past. ~ John Dryden

GRATITUDE FOR TOMORROW

_____ Daily # (After): _____

GRATITUDE TODAY

Day: _____

Date: _____

Daily # (Before): _____

Current Events/Special Occasion:

_____

_____

I am grateful for:

_____

_____

_____

_____

_____

_____

_____

The highlight or anticipated highlight for my day:

_____

_____

As each day comes to us refreshed and anew, so does my gratitude renew itself daily. ~ Terri Gauteet

GRATITUDE FOR TOMORROW

_____ Daily # (After): _____

GRATITUDE TODAY

Day: _____

Date: _____

Daily # (Before): _____

Current Events/Special Occasion:

_____

_____

I am grateful for:

_____

_____

_____

_____

_____

_____

_____

_____

The highlight or anticipated highlight for my day:

_____

_____

I would maintain that thanks are the highest form of thought; and that gratitude is happiness doubled by wonder. ~ G. K. Chesterton

GRATITUDE FOR TOMORROW

_____ Daily # (After): _____

GRATITUDE TODAY

Day: _____

Date: _____

Daily # (Before): _____

Current Events/Special Occasion:

_____

_____

I am grateful for:

_____

_____

_____

_____

_____

_____

_____

_____

The highlight or anticipated highlight for my day:

_____

_____

Feeling gratitude and not expressing it is like wrapping a present and not giving it. ~ William Arthur Ward

GRATITUDE FOR TOMORROW

_____ Daily # (After). _____

GRATITUDE TODAY

Day: _____

Date: _____

Daily # (Before): _____

Current Events/Special Occasion:

_____

_____

I am grateful for:

_____

_____

_____

_____

_____

_____

_____

The highlight or anticipated highlight for my day:

_____

_____

If a fellow isn't thankful for what he's got, he isn't likely to be thankful for what he's going to get. ~ Frank A. Clark

GRATITUDE FOR TOMORROW

_____ Daily # (After): _____

GRATITUDE TODAY

Day: _____

Date: _____

Daily # (Before): _____

Current Events/Special Occasion:

_____

_____

I am grateful for:

_____

_____

_____

_____

_____

_____

_____

_____

The highlight or anticipated highlight for my day:

_____

_____

The unthankful heart... discovers no mercies; but let the thankful heart sweep through the day and, as the magnet finds the iron, so it will find, in every hour, some heavenly blessings! ~ Henry Ward Beecher

GRATITUDE FOR TOMORROW

_____ Daily # (After): _____

GRATITUDE TODAY

Day: _____

Date: _____

Daily # (Before): _____

Current Events/Special Occasion:

_____

_____

I am grateful for:

_____

_____

_____

_____

_____

_____

_____

The highlight or anticipated highlight for my day:

_____

_____

Grace isn't a little prayer you chant before receiving a meal. It's a way to live. ~ Attributed to Jacqueline Winspear

GRATITUDE FOR TOMORROW

_____ Daily # (After): _____

GRATITUDE TODAY

Day: _____

Date: _____

Daily # (Before): _____

Current Events/Special Occasion:

_____

_____

I am grateful for:

_____

_____

_____

_____

_____

_____

_____

The highlight or anticipated highlight for my day:

_____

_____

Praise the bridge that carried you over. ~ George Colman

GRATITUDE FOR TOMORROW

_____ Daily # (After): _____

GRATITUDE TODAY

Day: _____

Date: _____

Daily # (Before): _____

Current Events/Special Occasion:

_____

_____

I am grateful for:

_____

_____

_____

_____

_____

_____

_____

_____

The highlight or anticipated highlight for my day:

_____

_____

If you count all your assets, you always show a profit. ~ Robert Quillen

GRATITUDE FOR TOMORROW

_____ Daily # (After): _____

GRATITUDE TODAY

Day: _____

Date: _____

Daily # (Before): _____

Current Events/Special Occasion:

_____

_____

I am grateful for:

_____

_____

_____

_____

_____

_____

_____

_____

The highlight or anticipated highlight for my day:

_____

_____

He is a wise man who does not grieve for the things which he has not, but rejoices for those which he has. ~ Epictetus

GRATITUDE FOR TOMORROW

_____ Daily # (After): _____

GRATITUDE TODAY

Day: _____

Date: _____

Daily # (Before): _____

Current Events/Special Occasion:

_____

_____

I am grateful for:

_____

_____

_____

_____

_____

_____

_____

_____

The highlight or anticipated highlight for my day:

_____

_____

What a miserable thing life is: you're living in clover, only the clover isn't good enough. ~ Bertolt Brecht, Jungle of Cities, 1924

GRATITUDE FOR TOMORROW

_____ Daily # (After): _____

GRATITUDE TODAY

Day: _____

Date: _____

Daily # (Before): _____

Current Events/Special Occasion:

_____

_____

I am grateful for:

_____

_____

_____

_____

_____

_____

_____

_____

The highlight or anticipated highlight for my day:

_____

_____

Gratitude is the best attitude. ~ Author Unknown

GRATITUDE FOR TOMORROW

_____ Daily # (After): _____

GRATITUDE TODAY

Day: _____

Date: _____

Daily # (Before): _____

Current Events/Special Occasion:

_____

_____

I am grateful for:

_____

_____

_____

_____

_____

_____

_____

The highlight or anticipated highlight for my day:

_____

_____

Not what we say about our blessings, but how we use them, is the true measure of our thanksgiving. ~ W.T. Purkiser

GRATITUDE FOR TOMORROW

_____ Daily # (After): _____

GRATITUDE TODAY

Day: _____

Date: _____

Daily # (Before): _____

Current Events/Special Occasion:

_____

_____

I am grateful for:

_____

_____

_____

_____

_____

_____

_____

_____

The highlight or anticipated highlight for my day:

_____

_____

We thank Thee, O Father of all, for… all the soul-help that sad souls understand.
~ Will Carleton

GRATITUDE FOR TOMORROW

_____ Daily # (After): _____

GRATITUDE TODAY

Day: _____

Date: _____

Daily # (Before): _____

Current Events/Special Occasion:

_____

_____

I am grateful for:

_____

_____

_____

_____

_____

_____

_____

_____

The highlight or anticipated highlight for my day:

_____

_____

We can only be said to be alive in those moments when our hearts are conscious of our treasures. ~ Thornton Wilder

GRATITUDE FOR TOMORROW

_____ Daily # (After): _____

GRATITUDE TODAY

Day: _____

Date: _____

Daily # (Before): _____

Current Events/Special Occasion:

_____

_____

I am grateful for:

_____

_____

_____

_____

_____

_____

_____

_____

The highlight or anticipated highlight for my day:

_____

_____

Gratitude is a quality similar to electricity: it must be produced and discharged and used up in order to exist at all. ~ William Faulkner

GRATITUDE FOR TOMORROW

_____ Daily # (After): _____

GRATITUDE TODAY

Day: _____

Date: _____

Daily # (Before): _____

Current Events/Special Occasion:

_____

_____

I am grateful for:

_____

_____

_____

_____

_____

_____

_____

_____

The highlight or anticipated highlight for my day:

_____

_____

If you want to turn your life around, try thankfulness. It will change your life mightily. ~ Gerald Good

GRATITUDE FOR TOMORROW

_____ Daily # (After): _____

GRATITUDE TODAY

Day: _____

Date: _____

Daily # (Before): _____

Current Events/Special Occasion:

_____

_____

I am grateful for:

_____

_____

_____

_____

_____

_____

_____

_____

The highlight or anticipated highlight for my day:

_____

_____

Gratitude is the least of the virtues, but ingratitude is the worst of vices.
~ Thomas Fuller

GRATITUDE FOR TOMORROW

_____ Daily # (After): _____

GRATITUDE TODAY

Day: _____

Date: _____

Daily # (Before): _____

Current Events/Special Occasion:

_____

_____

I am grateful for:

_____

_____

_____

_____

_____

_____

_____

The highlight or anticipated highlight for my day:

_____

_____

There is not a more pleasing exercise of the mind than gratitude. It is accompanied with such an inward satisfaction that the duty is done.
~ Joseph Addison

GRATITUDE FOR TOMORROW

_____ Daily # (After): _____

GRATITUDE TODAY

Day: _____

Date: _____

Daily # (Before): _____

Current Events/Special Occasion:

_____

_____

I am grateful for:

_____

_____

_____

_____

_____

_____

_____

The highlight or anticipated highlight for my day:

_____

_____

I feel a very unusual sensation - if it is not indigestion, I think it must be gratitude. ~ Benjamin Disraeli

GRATITUDE FOR TOMORROW

_____ Daily # (After): _____

GRATITUDE TODAY

Day: _____

Date: _____

Daily # (Before): _____

Current Events/Special Occasion:

_____

_____

I am grateful for:

_____

_____

_____

_____

_____

_____

_____

_____

The highlight or anticipated highlight for my day:

_____

_____

There is no greater difference between men than between grateful and ungrateful people. ~ R. H. Blyth

GRATITUDE FOR TOMORROW

_____ Daily # (After): _____

GRATITUDE TODAY

Day: _____

Date: _____

Daily # (Before): _____

Current Events/Special Occasion:

_____

_____

I am grateful for:

_____

_____

_____

_____

_____

_____

_____

_____

The highlight or anticipated highlight for my day:

_____

_____

Courtesies of a small and trivial character are the ones which strike deepest in the grateful and appreciating heart. ~ H. Clay

GRATITUDE FOR TOMORROW

_____ Daily # (After): _____

GRATITUDE TODAY

Day: _____

Date: _____

Daily # (Before): _____

Current Events/Special Occasion:

_____

_____

I am grateful for:

_____

_____

_____

_____

_____

_____

_____

_____

The highlight or anticipated highlight for my day:

_____

_____

Who does not thank for little will not thank for much. ~ Estonian Proverb

GRATITUDE FOR TOMORROW

_____ Daily # (After): _____

GRATITUDE TODAY

Day: _____

Date: _____

Daily # (Before): _____

Current Events/Special Occasion:

_____

_____

I am grateful for:

_____

_____

_____

_____

_____

_____

_____

_____

The highlight or anticipated highlight for my day:

_____

_____

All that we behold is full of blessings. ~ William Wordsworth

GRATITUDE FOR TOMORROW

_____ Daily # (After): _____

GRATITUDE TODAY

Day: _____

Date: _____

Daily # (Before): _____

Current Events/Special Occasion:

_____

_____

I am grateful for:

_____

_____

_____

_____

_____

_____

_____

The highlight or anticipated highlight for my day:

_____

_____

The hardest arithmetic to master is that which enables us to count our blessings.
~ Eric Hoffer

GRATITUDE FOR TOMORROW

_____ Daily # (After): _____

GRATITUDE TODAY

Day: _____

Date: _____

Daily # (Before): _____

Current Events/Special Occasion:

_____

_____

I am grateful for:

_____

_____

_____

_____

_____

_____

_____

_____

The highlight or anticipated highlight for my day:

_____

_____

Gratitude is the fairest blossom which springs from the soul. ~ Henry Ward Beecher

GRATITUDE FOR TOMORROW

_____ Daily # (After): _____

GRATITUDE TODAY

Day: _____

Date: _____

Daily # (Before): _____

Current Events/Special Occasion:

_____

_____

I am grateful for:

_____

_____

_____

_____

_____

_____

_____

_____

_____

The highlight or anticipated highlight for my day:

_____

_____

When our perils are past, shall our gratitude sleep? ~ George Canning

GRATITUDE FOR TOMORROW

_____ Daily # (After): _____

GRATITUDE TODAY

Day: _____

Date: _____

Daily # (Before): _____

Current Events/Special Occasion:

_____

_____

I am grateful for:

_____

_____

_____

_____

_____

_____

_____

The highlight or anticipated highlight for my day:

_____

_____

As we express our gratitude, we must never forget that the highest appreciation is not to utter words, but to live by them. ~ J. F. Kennedy

GRATITUDE FOR TOMORROW

_____ Daily # (After): _____

GRATITUDE TODAY

Day: _____

Date: _____

Daily # (Before): _____

Current Events/Special Occasion:

_____

_____

I am grateful for:

_____

_____

_____

_____

_____

_____

_____

_____

The highlight or anticipated highlight for my day:

_____

_____

We often take for granted the very things that most deserve our gratitude.
~ Cynthia Ozick

GRATITUDE FOR TOMORROW

_____ Daily # (After): _____

GRATITUDE TODAY

Day: _____

Date: _____

Daily # (Before): _____

Current Events/Special Occasion:

_____

_____

I am grateful for:

_____

_____

_____

_____

_____

_____

_____

The highlight or anticipated highlight for my day:

_____

_____

The grateful person, being still the most severe exacter of himself, not only confesses, but proclaims, his debts. ~ R. South

GRATITUDE FOR TOMORROW

_____ Daily # (After): _____

GRATITUDE TODAY

Day: _____

Date: _____

Daily # (Before): _____

Current Events/Special Occasion:

_____

_____

I am grateful for:

_____

_____

_____

_____

_____

_____

_____

_____

The highlight or anticipated highlight for my day:

_____

_____

Gratitude is merely the secret hope of further favors. ~ François Duc de La Rochefoucauld

GRATITUDE FOR TOMORROW

_____ Daily # (After): _____

GRATITUDE TODAY

Day: _____

Date: _____

Daily # (Before): _____

Current Events/Special Occasion:

_____

_____

I am grateful for:

_____

_____

_____

_____

_____

_____

_____

The highlight or anticipated highlight for my day:

_____

_____

Most human beings have an almost infinite capacity for taking things for granted. ~ Aldous Huxley

GRATITUDE FOR TOMORROW

_____ Daily # (After): _____

GRATITUDE TODAY

Day: _____

Date: _____

Daily # (Before): _____

Current Events/Special Occasion:

_____

_____

I am grateful for:

_____

_____

_____

_____

_____

_____

_____

_____

The highlight or anticipated highlight for my day:

_____

_____

Hem your blessings with thankfulness so they don't unravel. ~ Author Unknown

GRATITUDE FOR TOMORROW

_____ Daily # (After): _____

GRATITUDE TODAY

Day: _____

Date: _____

Daily # (Before): _____

Current Events/Special Occasion:

_____

_____

I am grateful for:

_____

_____

_____

_____

_____

_____

_____

The highlight or anticipated highlight for my day:

_____

_____

God gave you a gift of 86,400 seconds today. Have you used one to say "Thank you?" ~ William A. Ward

GRATITUDE FOR TOMORROW

_____ Daily # (After): _____

GRATITUDE TODAY

Day: _____

Date: _____

Daily # (Before): _____

Current Events/Special Occasion:

_____

_____

I am grateful for:

_____

_____

_____

_____

_____

_____

_____

The highlight or anticipated highlight for my day:

_____

_____

Gratitude makes sense of our past, brings peace for today, and creates a vision for tomorrow. ~ Melody Beattie

GRATITUDE FOR TOMORROW

_____ Daily # (After): _____

GRATITUDE TODAY

Day: _____

Date: _____

Daily # (Before): _____

Current Events/Special Occasion:

_____

_____

I am grateful for:

_____

_____

_____

_____

_____

_____

_____

_____

The highlight or anticipated highlight for my day:

_____

_____

I am full of gratitude for my life - and for this house. ~ J. Clary

GRATITUDE FOR TOMORROW

_____ Daily # (After): _____

ABOUT THE AUTHOR

David George Brooke – That Gratitude Guy has been a speaker, teacher, coach, and best-selling author for over 30 years. He specializes in coaching people to cope with and manage the stresses of life by applying an attitude of gratitude. To access his strategies on how to utilize your Daily Gratitude Journal, and to order additional copies, visit his website:

www.thatgratitudeguy.com

Made in the USA
Monee, IL
28 June 2021